This Book Belongs To:

_____

_____

A Child's Garden of Verses

ROBERT LOUIS STEVENSON
Illustrated by T. Lewis

A CALICO BOOK
Published by Contemporary Books, Inc.
CHICAGO · NEW YORK

Library of Congress Cataloging-in-Publication Data

Stevenson, Robert Louis, 1850–1894.
[Child's garden of verses]
A calico child's garden of verses / Robert Louis Stevenson ;
illustrated by T. Lewis.
p.   cm.
Originally published as: A child's garden of verses.
"A Calico book."
Summary: A collection of poems evoking the world and feelings of
childhood.
ISBN 0-8092-4356-3
1. Children's poetry, Scottish.   [1. English poetry.]   I. Title.
PR54789.C5   1989b
821'.8—dc19   88-36788
                                                                    CIP
                                                                    AC

Copyright © 1989 by The Kipling Press
Illustrations copyright © 1989 by T. Lewis
Border illustrations copyright © 1989 by Sara Gutiérrez
Border design copyright © 1989 by Yvonne Collery
Designed by Yvonne Collery
Art Editing by Charlotte Krebs
All rights reserved
Published by Contemporary Books, Inc.
180 North Michigan Avenue, Chicago, Illinois 60601
Manufactured in the United States of America
International Standard Book Number: 0-8092-4356-3

Published simultaneously in Canada by Beaverbooks, Ltd.
195 Allstate Parkway, Valleywood Business Park
Markham, Ontario L3R 4T8 Canada

*To Jodfrey and Chantelle
and the summer of 1988
—T. Lewis*

TABLE OF CONTENTS

INTRODUCTION

Robert Louis Stevenson spent the summer of 1881 visiting his parents in their damp Highland home in Braemar, Scotland. There, at the age of thirty-one, Stevenson began writing not only his classic novel *Treasure Island* but also a series of poems about his childhood. Four years later these verses were collected and published, and to this day *A Child's Garden of Verses* is recognized as one of the most notable books of poems for children ever written.

In *A Child's Garden of Verses*, Stevenson recaptured his early years spent in Edinburgh in the 1850s. Though he'd been an isolated only child and had suffered from chronic chest problems, the cheerful tone of his verses reflects a happy childhood. Perhaps this can be attributed partly to his nurse, Alison Cunningham, to whom he dedicated the book. She is the "nursie" with whom Stevenson gathers treasures and spends "happy, chimney-corner days" under her tender care, in the upper-class atmosphere of "great and cool rooms."

The children of Stevenson's poems live imaginative lives. They believe in fairies and travel freely and spontaneously to the Land of Counterpane, the Land of Storybooks, and the Land of Nod. They shut their eyes "to go sailing far away to the pleasant Land of Play." They let "the sofa be mountains, the carpet be sea." And when they travel at night through the stars, the Dog, the Plow, and the Hunter chase them back to bed.

The verses in this collection have an old-fashioned British flavor and tone—from the lamplighter making his rounds at teatime to the organ-grinder singing in the rain. American readers may not know that "wicket" means a garden arch, that a "kirk" is a church building, or that the word "gabies" in "Nest Eggs" and "Good and Bad Children" is an archaic British term for simpletons.

Even though *A Child's Garden of Verses* represents a world quite different from ours today, readers of all generations seem to recognize Stevenson's territory as soon as they cross its threshold. It's as if a secret child within all of us lives there still. Stevenson himself acknowledges that child:

> As from the house your mother sees
> You playing round the garden trees,
> So you may see, if you will look
> Through the windows of this book,
> Another child, far, far away . . . .

That inner child—that child of air who still "lingers in the garden there"—is animated anew each time we enter *A Child's Garden of Verses*.

Mary Pope Osborne

TO ANY READER

As from the house your mother sees
  You playing round the garden trees,
So you may see, if you will look
  Through the windows of this book,
Another child, far, far away,
  And in another garden, play.
But do not think you can at all,
  By knocking on the window, call
That child to hear you. He intent
  Is all on his play-business bent.
He does not hear; he will not look,
  Nor yet be lured out of this book.
For, long ago, the truth to say,
  He has grown up and gone away,
And it is but a child of air
  That lingers in the garden there.

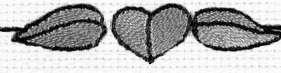

BED IN SUMMER

In winter I get up at night
    And dress by yellow candlelight.
In summer, quite the other way,
    I have to go to bed by day.

I have to go to bed and see
    The birds still hopping on the tree,
Or hear the grown-up people's feet
    Still going past me in the street.

And does it not seem hard to you,
    When all the sky is clear and blue,
And I should like so much to play,
    To have to go to bed by day?

WHOLE DUTY OF CHILDREN

A child should always say what's true
  And speak when he is spoken to,
And behave mannerly at table;
  At least as far as he is able.

RAIN

The rain is raining all around,
  It falls on field and tree,
It rains on the umbrellas here,
  And on the ships at sea.

YOUNG NIGHT THOUGHT

All night long and every night,
   When my mama puts out the light,
I see the people marching by,
   As plain as day, before my eye.

Armies and emperors and kings,
   All carrying different kinds of things,
And marching in so grand a way,
   You never saw the like by day.

So fine a show was never seen
   At the great circus on the green;
For every kind of beast and man
   Is marching in that caravan.

At first they move a little slow,
   But still the faster on they go,
And still beside them close I keep
   Until we reach the Town of Sleep.

PIRATE STORY

Three of us afloat in the meadow by the swing,
  Three of us aboard in the basket on the lea.
Winds are in the air, they are blowing in the spring,
  And waves are on the meadow like the waves there are at sea.

Where shall we adventure, today that we're afloat,
  Wary of the weather and steering by a star?
Shall it be to Africa, a-steering of the boat,
  To Providence, or Babylon, or off to Malabar?

Hi! but here's a squadron a-rowing on the sea—
  Cattle on the meadow a-charging with a roar!
Quick, and we'll escape them, they're as mad as they can be,
  The wicket is the harbor and the garden is the shore.

FOREIGN LANDS

Up into the cherry tree
    Who should climb but little me?
I held the trunk with both my hands
    And looked abroad on foreign lands.

I saw the next-door garden lie,
    Adorned with flowers, before my eye,
And many pleasant places more
    That I had never seen before.

I saw the dimpling river pass
    And be the sky's blue looking glass;
The dusty roads go up and down
    With people tramping into town.

If I could find a higher tree
    Farther and farther I should see,
To where the grown-up river slips
    Into the sea among the ships,

To where the roads on either hand
    Lead onward into fairy land,
Where all the children dine at five,
    And all the playthings come alive.

SINGING

Of speckled eggs the birdie sings
   And nests among the trees;
The sailor sings of ropes and things
   In ships upon the seas.

The children sing in far Japan,
   The children sing in Spain;
The organ with the organ man
   Is singing in the rain.

AT THE SEASIDE

When I was down beside the sea
   A wooden spade they gave to me
   To dig the sandy shore.

My holes were empty like a cup.
   In every hole the sea came up,
   Till it could come no more.

LOOKING FORWARD

When I am grown to man's estate
I shall be very proud and great,
And tell the other girls and boys
Not to meddle with my toys.

A GOOD PLAY

We built a ship upon the stairs
  All made of the back-bedroom chairs,
And filled it full of sofa pillows
  To go a-sailing on the billows.

We took a saw and several nails,
  And water in the nursery pails;
And Tom said, "Let us also take
  An apple and a slice of cake"—
Which was enough for Tom and me
  To go a-sailing on, till tea.

We sailed along for days and days,
  And had the very best of plays;
But Tom fell out and hurt his knee,
  So there was no one left but me.

BLOCK CITY

What are you able to build with your blocks?
　　Castles and palaces, temples and docks.
Rain may keep raining, and others go roam,
　　But I can be happy and building at home.

Let the sofa be mountains, the carpet be sea,
　　There I'll establish a city for me:
A kirk and a mill and a palace beside,
　　And a harbor as well where my vessels may ride.

Great is the palace with pillar and wall,
　　A sort of a tower on the top of it all,
And steps coming down in an orderly way
　　To where my toy vessels lie safe in the bay.

This one is sailing and that one is moored:
　　Hark to the song of the sailors on board!
And see on the steps of my palace, the kings
　　Coming and going with presents and things!

Now I have done with it, down let it go!
　　All in a moment the town is laid low.
Block upon block lying scattered and free,
　　What is there left of my town by the sea?

Yet as I saw it, I see it again,
　　The kirk and the palace, the ships and the men,
And as long as I live and where'er I may be,
　　I'll always remember my town by the sea.

WHERE GO THE BOATS?

Dark brown is the river,
    Golden is the sand.
It flows along forever,
    With trees on either hand.

Green leaves a-floating,
    Castles of the foam,
Boats of mine a-boating—
    Where will all come home?

On goes the river
    And out past the mill,
Away down the valley,
    Away down the hill.

Away down the river,
    A hundred miles or more,
Other little children
    Shall bring my boats ashore.

AUNTIE'S SKIRTS

Whenever Auntie moves around,
　　Her dresses make a curious sound;
They trail behind her up the floor,
　　And trundle after through the door.

THE LAND OF NOD

From breakfast on through all the day
 At home among my friends I stay,
But every night I go abroad
 Afar into the Land of Nod.

All by myself I have to go,
 With none to tell me what to do—
All alone beside the streams
 And up the mountainsides of dreams.

The strangest things are there for me,
 Both things to eat and things to see,
And many frightening sights abroad
 Till morning in the Land of Nod.

Try as I like to find the way,
 I never can get back by day,
Nor can remember plain and clear
 The curious music that I hear.

MY SHADOW

I have a little shadow that goes in and out with me,
   And what can be the use of him is more than I can see.
He is very, very like me from the heels up to the head;
   And I see him jump before me, when I jump into my bed.

The funniest thing about him is the way he likes to grow—
   Not at all like proper children, which is always very slow;
For he sometimes shoots up taller like an india-rubber ball,
   And he sometimes gets so little that there's none of him at all.

He hasn't got a notion of how children ought to play,
   And can only make a fool of me in every sort of way.
He stays so close beside me, he's a coward you can see;
   I'd think shame to stick to nursie as that shadow sticks to me!

One morning, very early, before the sun was up,
   I rose and found the shining dew on every buttercup;
But my lazy little shadow, like an arrant sleepyhead,
   Had stayed at home behind me and was fast asleep in bed.

THE LAND OF COUNTERPANE

When I was sick and lay abed,
  I had two pillows at my head,
And all my toys beside me lay
  To keep me happy all the day.

And sometimes for an hour or so
  I watched my leaden soldiers go,
With different uniforms and drills,
  Among the bedclothes, through the hills.

And sometimes sent my ships in fleets
  All up and down among the sheets;
Or brought my trees and houses out,
  And planted cities all about.

I was the giant great and still
  That sits upon the pillow hill,
And sees before him, dale and plain,
  The pleasant Land of Counterpane.

SYSTEM

Every night my prayers I say,
    And get my dinner every day;
And every day that I've been good,
    I get an orange after food.

The child that is not clean and neat,
    With lots of toys and things to eat,
He is a naughty child, I'm sure—
    Or else his dear papa is poor.

A GOOD BOY

I woke before the morning, I was happy all the day,
    I never said an ugly word, but smiled and stuck to play.

And now at last the sun is going down behind the wood,
    And I am very happy, for I know that I've been good.

My bed is waiting cool and fresh, with linen smooth and fair,
    And I must off to sleepsin-by, and not forget my prayer.

I know that, till tomorrow I shall see the sun arise,
    No ugly dream shall fright my mind, no ugly sight my eyes.

But slumber hold me tightly till I waken in the dawn,
    And hear the thrushes singing in the lilacs round the lawn.

ESCAPE AT BEDTIME

The lights from the parlor and kitchen shone out
  Through the blinds and the windows and bars;
And high overhead and all moving about,
  There were thousands of millions of stars.
There ne'er were such thousands of leaves on a tree,
  Nor of people in church or the park,
As the crowds of the stars that looked down upon me,
  And that glittered and winked in the dark.

The Dog, and the Plow, and the Hunter, and all,
  And the star of the sailor, and Mars,
These shone in the sky, and the pail by the wall
  Would be half-full of water and stars.
They saw me at last, and they chased me with cries,
  And they soon had me packed into bed;
But the glory kept shining and bright in my eyes,
  And the stars going round in my head.

MARCHING SONG

Bring the comb and play upon it!
   Marching, here we come!
Willie cocks his highland bonnet,
   Johnnie beats the drum.

Mary Jane commands the party,
   Peter leads the rear;
Feet in time, alert and hearty,
   Each a grenadier!

All in the most martial manner
   Marching double-quick;
While the napkin like a banner
   Waves upon the stick!

Here's enough of fame and pillage,
   Great commander Jane!
Now that we've been round the village,
   Let's go home again.

THE COW

The friendly cow all red and white,
  I love with all my heart:
She gives me cream with all her might,
  To eat with apple tart.

She wanders lowing here and there,
  And yet she cannot stray,
All in the pleasant open air,
  The pleasant light of day;

And blown by all the winds that pass
  And wet with all the showers,
She walks among the meadow grass
  And eats the meadow flowers.

THE WIND

I saw you toss the kites on high
  And blow the birds about the sky;
And all around I heard you pass,
  Like ladies' skirts across the grass—
    O wind, a-blowing all day long,
    O wind, that sings so loud a song!

I saw the different things you did,
  But always you yourself you hid.
I felt you push, I heard you call,
  I could not see yourself at all—
    O wind, a-blowing all day long,
    O wind, that sings so loud a song!

O you that are so strong and cold,
  O blower, are you young or old?
Are you a beast of field and tree,
  Or just a stronger child than me?
    O wind, a-blowing all day long,
    O wind, that sings so loud a song!

GOOD AND BAD CHILDREN

Children, you are very little,
   And your bones are very brittle;
If you would grow great and stately,
   You must try to walk sedately.

You must still be bright and quiet,
   And content with simple diet;
And remain, through all bewild'ring,
   Innocent and honest children.

Happy hearts and happy faces,
   Happy play in grassy places—
That was how, in ancient ages,
   Children grew to kings and sages.

But the unkind and the unruly,
   And the sort who eat unduly,
They must never hope for glory—
   Theirs is quite a different story!

Cruel children, crying babies,
   All grow up as geese and gabies,
Hated, as their age increases,
   By their nephews and their nieces.

FROM A RAILWAY CARRIAGE

Faster than fairies, faster than witches,
  Bridges and houses, hedges and ditches;
And charging along like troops in a battle,
  All through the meadows the horses and cattle:
All of the sights of the hill and the plain
  Fly as thick as driving rain;
And ever again, in the wink of an eye,
  Painted stations whistle by.

Here is a child who clambers and scrambles,
  All by himself and gathering brambles;
Here is a tramp who stands and gazes;
  And there is the green for stringing the daisies!
Here is a cart run away in the road
  Lumping along with man and load;
And here is a mill and there is a river:
  Each a glimpse and gone forever!

THE LAMPLIGHTER

My tea is nearly ready and the sun has left the sky;
  It's time to take the window to see Leerie going by;
For every night at teatime and before you take your seat,
  With lantern and with ladder he comes posting up the street.

Now Tom would be a driver and Maria go to sea,
  And my papa's a banker and as rich as he can be;
But I, when I am stronger and can choose what I'm to do,
  O Leerie, I'll go round at night and light the lamps with you!

For we are very lucky, with a lamp before the door,
  And Leerie stops to light it as he lights so many more;
And O! before you hurry by with ladder and with light,
  O Leerie, see a little child and nod to him tonight!

THE SUN'S TRAVELS

The sun is not abed, when I
   At night upon my pillow lie;
Still round the earth his way he takes,
   And morning after morning makes.

While here at home, in shining day,
   We round the sunny garden play,
Each little Indian sleepyhead
   Is being kissed and put to bed.

And when at eve I rise from tea,
   Day dawns beyond the Atlantic Sea;
And all the children in the West
   Are getting up and being dressed.

MY BED IS A BOAT

My bed is like a little boat;
  Nurse helps me in when I embark;
She girds me in my sailor's coat
  And starts me in the dark.

At night, I go on board and say
  Good night to all my friends on shore;
I shut my eyes and sail away
  And see and hear no more.

And sometimes things to bed I take,
  As prudent sailors have to do;
Perhaps a slice of wedding cake,
  Perhaps a toy or two.

All night across the dark we steer;
  But when the day returns at last,
Safe in my room, beside the pier,
  I find my vessel fast.

THE HAYLOFT

Through all the pleasant meadowside
  The grass grew shoulder-high,
Till the shining scythes went far and wide
  And cut it down to dry.

These green and sweetly smelling crops
  They led in wagons home;
And they piled them here in mountaintops
  For mountaineers to roam.

Here is Mount Clear, Mount Rusty-Nail,
  Mount Eagle and Mount High;—
The mice that in these mountains dwell,
  No happier are than I!

O what a joy to clamber there,
  O what a place for play,
With the sweet, the dim, the dusty air,
  The happy hills of hay!

THE MOON

The moon has a face like the clock in the hall;
   She shines on thieves on the garden wall,
On streets and fields and harbor quays,
   And birdies asleep in the forks of the trees.

The squalling cat and the squeaking mouse,
   The howling dog by the door of the house,
The bat that lies in bed at noon,
   All love to be out by the light of the moon.

But all of the things that belong to the day
   Cuddle to sleep to be out of her way;
And flowers and children close their eyes
   Till up in the morning the sun shall arise.

THE SWING

How do you like to go up in a swing,
　Up in the air so blue?
Oh, I do think it the pleasantest thing
　Ever a child can do!

Up in the air and over the wall,
　Till I can see so wide,
Rivers and trees and cattle and all
　Over the countryside—

Till I look down on the garden green,
　Down on the roof so brown—
Up in the air I go flying again,
　Up in the air and down!

TIME TO RISE

A birdie with a yellow bill
  Hopped upon the windowsill,
Cocked his shining eye and said:
  "Ain't you 'shamed, you sleepyhead!"

LOOKING-GLASS RIVER

Smooth it slides upon its travel,
  Here a wimple, there a gleam—
    O the clean gravel!
    O the smooth stream!

Sailing blossoms, silver fishes,
  Paven pools as clear as air—
    How a child wishes
    To live down there!

We can see our colored faces
  Floating on the shaken pool
    Down in cool places,
    Dim and very cool;

Till a wind or water wrinkle,
  Dipping marten, plumping trout,
    Spreads in a twinkle
    And blots all out.

See the rings pursue each other;
  All below grows black as night,
    Just as if mother
    Had blown out the light!

Patience, children, just a minute—
  See the spreading circles die;
    The stream and all in it
    Will clear by-and-by.

FAIRY BREAD

Come up here, O dusty feet!
    Here is fairy bread to eat.
Here in my retiring room,
    Children, you may dine
On the golden smell of broom
    And the shade of pine;
And when you have eaten well,
    Fairy stories hear and tell.

WINTERTIME

Late lies the wintry sun abed,
 A frosty, fiery sleepyhead;
Blinks but an hour or two; and then,
 A blood-red orange, sets again.

Before the stars have left the skies,
 At morning in the dark I rise;
And shivering in my nakedness,
 By the cold candle, bathe and dress.

Close by the jolly fire I sit
 To warm my frozen bones a bit;
Or with a reindeer sled, explore
 The colder countries round the door.

When to go out, my nurse doth wrap
 Me in my comforter and cap;
The cold wind burns my face, and blows
 Its frosty pepper up my nose.

Black are my steps on silver sod;
 Thick blows my frosty breath abroad;
And tree and house, and hill and lake,
 Are frosted like a wedding cake.

FAREWELL TO THE FARM

The coach is at the door at last;
   The eager children, mounting fast
And kissing hands, in chorus sing:
   Good-bye, good-bye, to everything!

To house and garden, field and lawn,
   The meadow-gates we swang upon,
To pump and stable, tree and swing,
   Good-bye, good-bye, to everything!

And fare you well for evermore,
   O ladder at the hayloft door,
O hayloft where the cobwebs cling,
   Good-bye, good-bye, to everything!

Crack goes the whip, and off we go;
   The trees and houses smaller grow;
Last, round the woody turn we swing:
   Good-bye, good-bye, to everything!

NORTHWEST PASSAGE

1. Good Night

When the bright lamp is carried in,
 The sunless hours again begin;
O'er all without, in field and lane,
 The haunted night returns again.

Now we behold the embers flee
 About the firelit hearth; and see
Our faces painted as we pass,
 Like pictures, on the window-glass.

Must we to bed indeed? Well then,
 Let us arise and go like men,
And face with an undaunted tread
 The long black passage up to bed.

Farewell, O brother, sister, sire!
 O pleasant party round the fire!
The songs you sing, the tales you tell,
 Till far tomorrow, fare ye well!

2. Shadow March

All round the house is the jet-black night;
 It stares through the windowpane;
It crawls in the corners, hiding from the light,
 And it moves with the moving flame.

Now my little heart goes a-beating like a drum,
 With the breath of the bogey in my hair;
And all round the candle the crooked shadows come,
 And go marching along up the stair.

The shadow of the balusters, the shadow of the lamp,
 The shadow of the child that goes to bed—
All the wicked shadows coming, tramp, tramp, tramp,
 With the black night overhead.

3. In Port

Last, to the chamber where I lie
  My fearful footsteps patter nigh,
And come from out the cold and gloom
  Into my warm and cheerful room.

There, safe arrived, we turn about
  To keep the coming shadows out,
And close the happy door at last
  On all the perils that we past.

Then, when Mama goes by to bed,
  She shall come in with tiptoe tread,
And see me lying warm and fast
  And in the Land of Nod at last.

THE UNSEEN PLAYMATE

When children are playing alone on the green,
  In comes the playmate that never was seen.
When children are happy and lonely and good,
  The Friend of the Children comes out of the wood.

Nobody heard him and nobody saw,
  His is a picture you never could draw,
But he's sure to be present, abroad or at home,
  When children are happy and playing alone.

He lies in the laurels, he runs on the grass,
  He sings when you tinkle the musical glass;
Whene'er you are happy and cannot tell why,
  The Friend of the Children is sure to be by!

He loves to be little, he hates to be big,
  'Tis he that inhabits the caves that you dig;
'Tis he when you play with your soldiers of tin
  That sides with the Frenchmen and never can win.

'Tis he, when at night you go off to your bed,
  Bids you go to your sleep and not trouble your head;
For wherever they're lying, in cupboard or shelf,
  'Tis he will take care of your playthings himself!

MY SHIP AND I

O it's I that am the captain of a tidy little ship,
  Of a ship that goes a-sailing on the pond;
And my ship it keeps a-turning all around and all about;
But when I'm a little older, I shall find the secret out
  How to send my vessel sailing on beyond.

For I mean to grow as little as the dolly at the helm,
  And the dolly I intend to come alive;
And with him beside to help me, it's a-sailing I shall go,
It's a-sailing on the water, when the jolly breezes blow
  And the vessel goes a divie-divie-dive.

O it's then you'll see me sailing through the rushes and the reeds,
  And you'll hear the water singing at the prow;
For beside the dolly sailor, I'm to voyage and explore,
To land upon the island where no dolly was before,
  And to fire the penny cannon in the bow.

MY KINGDOM

Down by a shining water well
  I found a very little dell,
    No higher than my head.
The heather and the gorse about
  In summer bloom were coming out,
    Some yellow and some red.

I called the little pool a sea;
  The little hills were big to me;
    For I am very small.
I made a boat, I made a town,
  I searched the caverns up and down,
    And named them one and all.

And all about was mine, I said,
  The little sparrows overhead,
    The little minnows too.
This was the world and I was king;
  For me the bees came by to sing,
    For me the swallows flew

I played there were no deeper seas,
  Nor any wider plains than these,
    Nor other kings than me.
At last I heard my mother call
  Out from the house at evenfall,
    To call me home to tea.

And I must rise and leave my dell,
  And leave my dimpled water well,
    And leave my heather blooms.
Alas! and as my home I neared,
  How very big my nurse appeared,
    How great and cool the rooms!

MY TREASURES

These nuts, that I keep in the back of the nest
  Where all my lead soldiers are lying at rest,
Were gathered in autumn by nursie and me
  In a wood with a well by the side of the sea.

This whistle we made (and how clearly it sounds!)
  By the side of a field at the end of the grounds.
Of a branch of a plane, with a knife of my own,
  It was nursie who made it, and nursie alone!

The stone, with the white and the yellow and gray,
  We discovered I cannot tell *how* far away;
And I carried it back although weary and cold,
  For though father denies it, I'm sure it is gold.

But of all my treasures the last is the king,
  For there's very few children possess such a thing;
And that is a chisel, both handle and blade,
  Which a man who was really a carpenter made.

WINDY NIGHTS

Whenever the moon and stars are set,
  Whenever the wind is high,
All night long in the dark and wet,
  A man goes riding by.
Late in the night when the fires are out,
Why does he gallop and gallop about?

Whenever the trees are crying aloud,
  And ships are tossed at sea,
By, on the highway, low and loud,
  By at the gallop goes he.
By at the gallop he goes, and then
By he comes back at the gallop again.

PICTURE BOOKS IN WINTER

Summer fading, winter comes—
  Frosty mornings, tingling thumbs,
Window robins, winter rooks,
  And the picture storybooks.

Water now is turned to stone
  Nurse and I can walk upon;
Still we find the flowing brooks
  In the picture storybooks.

All the pretty things put by,
  Wait upon the children's eye,
Sheep and shepherds, trees and crooks,
  In the picture storybooks.

We may see how all things are
  Seas and cities, near and far,
And the flying fairies' looks,
  In the picture storybooks.

How am I to sing your praise,
  Happy chimney-corner days,
Sitting safe in nursery nooks,
  Reading picture storybooks?

ARMIES IN THE FIRE

The lamps now glitter down the street;
   Faintly sound the falling feet;
And the blue even slowly falls
   About the garden trees and walls.

Now in the falling of the gloom
   The red fire paints the empty room:
And warmly on the roof it looks,
   And flickers on the backs of books.

Armies march by tower and spire
   Of cities blazing, in the fire;—
Till as I gaze with staring eyes,
   The armies fade, the luster dies.

Then once again the glow returns;
   Again the phantom city burns;
And down the red-hot valley, lo!
   The phantom armies marching go!

Blinking embers, tell me true
   Where are those armies marching to,
And what the burning city is
   That crumbles in your furnaces!

THE LAND OF STORYBOOKS

At evening when the lamp is lit,
    Around the fire my parents sit;
They sit at home and talk and sing,
    And do not play at anything.

Now, with my little gun, I crawl
    All in the dark along the wall,
And follow round the forest track
    Away behind the sofa back.

There, in the night, where none can spy,
    All in my hunter's camp I lie,
And play at books that I have read
    Till it is time to go to bed.

These are the hills, these are the woods,
    These are my starry solitudes;
And there the river by whose brink
    The roaring lions come to drink.

I see the others far away
    As if in firelit camp they lay,
And I, like to an Indian scout,
    Around their party prowled about.

So, when my nurse comes in for me,
    Home I return across the sea,
And go to bed with backward looks
    At my dear Land of Storybooks.

THE LITTLE LAND

When at home alone I sit
  And am very tired of it,
I have just to shut my eyes
  To go sailing through the skies—
To go sailing far away
  To the pleasant Land of Play;
To the fairy land afar
  Where the Little People are;
Where the clover-tops are trees,
  And the rain-pools are the seas,
And the leaves like little ships
  Sail about on tiny trips;
And above the daisy tree
  Through the grasses,
High o'erhead the Bumble Bee
  Hums and passes.

In that forest to and fro
  I can wander, I can go;
See the spider and the fly,
  And the ants go marching by
Carrying parcels with their feet
  Down the green and grassy street.
I can in the sorrel sit
  Where the ladybird alit.
I can climb the jointed grass;
  And on high
See the greater swallows pass
  In the sky,
And the round sun rolling by
  Heeding no such things as I.

Through that forest I can pass
  Till, as in a looking glass,
Humming fly and daisy tree
  And my tiny self I see,
Painted very clear and neat
  On the rain-pool at my feet.
Should a leaflet come to land
  Drifting near to where I stand,
Straight I'll board that tiny boat
  Round the rain-pool sea to float.

Little thoughtful creatures sit
  On the grassy coasts of it;
Little things with lovely eyes
  See me sailing with surprise.
Some are clad in armor green—
  (These have sure to battle been!)—
Some are pied with ev'ry hue,
  Black and crimson, gold and blue;
Some have wings and swift are gone;—
  But they all look kindly on.

When my eyes I once again
  Open, and see all things plain:
High bare walls, great bare floor;
  Great big knobs on drawer and door;
Great big people perched on chairs,
  Stitching tucks and mending tears,
Each a hill that I could climb,
  And talking nonsense all the time—
    O dear me,
    That I could be
A sailor on the rain-pool sea,
  A climber in the clover tree,
And just come back, a sleepyhead,
  Late at night to go to bed.

NEST EGGS

Birds all the sunny day
  Flutter and quarrel
Here in the arbor-like
  Tent of the laurel.

Here in the fork
  The brown nest is seated;
Four little blue eggs
  The mother keeps heated.

While we stand watching her,
  Staring like gabies,
Safe in each egg are the
  Bird's little babies.

Soon the frail eggs they shall
  Chip, and upspringing,
Make all the April woods
  Merry with singing.

Younger than we are,
  O children, and frailer,
Soon in blue air they'll be,
  Singer and sailor.

We, so much older,
  Taller and stronger,
We shall look down on the
  Birdies no longer.

They shall go flying
  With musical speeches
High overhead in the
  Tops of the beeches.

In spite of our wisdom
  And sensible talking,
We on our feet must go
  Plodding and walking.

THE FLOWERS

All the names I know from nurse:
    Gardener's garters, Shepherd's purse,
Bachelor's buttons, Lady's smock,
    And the Lady Hollyhock.

Fairy places, fairy things,
    Fairy woods where the wild bee wings,
Tiny trees for tiny dames—
    These must all be fairy names!

Tiny woods below whose boughs
    Shady fairies weave a house;
Tiny treetops, rose or thyme,
    Where the braver fairies climb!

Fair are grown-up people's trees,
    But the fairest woods are these;
Where if I were not so tall,
    I should live for good and all.

THE DUMB SOLDIER

When the grass was closely mown,
  Walking on the lawn alone,
In the turf a hole I found
  And hid a soldier underground.

Spring and daisies came apace;
  Grasses hide my hiding place;
Grasses run like a green sea
  O'er the lawn up to my knee.

Under grass alone he lies,
  Looking up with leaden eyes,
Scarlet coat and pointed gun,
  To the stars and to the sun.

When the grass is ripe like grain,
  When the scythe is stoned again,
When the lawn is shaven clear,
  Then my hole shall reappear.

I shall find him, never fear,
  I shall find my grenadier;

But for all that's gone and come,
  I shall find my soldier dumb.

He has lived, a little thing,
  In the grassy woods of spring;
Done, if he could tell me true,
  Just as I should like to do.

He has seen the starry hours
  And the springing of the flowers;
And the fairy things that pass
  In the forests of the grass.

In the silence he has heard
  Talking bee and ladybird,
And the butterfly has flown
  O'er him as he lay alone.

Not a word will he disclose,
  Not a word of all he knows.
I must lay him on the shelf,
  And make up the tale myself.

SUMMER SUN

Great is the sun, and wide he goes
  Through empty heaven without repose;
And in the blue and glowing days
  More thick than rain he showers his rays.

Though closer still the blinds we pull
  To keep the shady parlor cool,
Yet he will find a chink or two
  To slip his golden fingers through.

The dusty attic spider-clad
  He, through the keyhole, maketh glad;
And through the broken edge of tiles,
  Into the laddered hayloft smiles.

Meantime his golden face around
  He bares to all the garden ground,
And sheds a warm and glittering look
  Among the ivy's inmost nook.

Above the hills, along the blue,
  Round the bright air with footing true,
To please the child, to paint the rose,
  The gardener of the World, he goes.

AUTUMN FIRES

In the other gardens
  And all up the vale,
From the autumn bonfires
  See the smoke trail!

Pleasant summer over
  And all the summer flowers,
The red fire blazes,
  The gray smoke towers.

Sing a song of seasons!
  Something bright in all!
Flowers in the summer,
  Fires in the fall!

HAPPY THOUGHT

The world is so full of a number of things,
I'm sure we should all be as happy as kings.